Holt McDougal
Mathematics

Grade 8
Problem Solving
Workbook

HOLT McDOUGAL

HOUGHTON MIFFLIN HARCOURT

COMMON CORE

EDITION

Contents

Holt McDougal Mathematics

LESSON	
1	

Rational Numbers

Problem Solving: Rational Numbers

Write the correct answer.

1. Fill in the table below which shows the sizes of drill bits in a set.

2. Do the drill bit sizes convert to repeating or terminating decimals?

_____

13-Piece Drill Bit Set

Fraction	Decimal	Fraction	Decimal	Fraction	Decimal
$\frac{1}{4}$"		$\frac{11}{64}$"		$\frac{3}{32}$"	
$\frac{15}{64}$"		$\frac{5}{32}$"		$\frac{5}{64}$"	
$\frac{7}{32}$"		$\frac{9}{64}$"		$\frac{1}{16}$"	
$\frac{13}{64}$"		$\frac{1}{8}$"			
$\frac{3}{16}$"		$\frac{7}{64}$"			

Use the table at the right that lists the world's smallest nations. Choose the letter for the best answer.

3. What is the area of Vatican City expressed as a fraction in simplest form?

   A $\frac{8}{50}$

   B $\frac{4}{25}$

   C $\frac{17}{1000}$

   D $\frac{17}{100}$

4. What is the area of Monaco expressed as a fraction in simplest form?

   F $\frac{75}{100}$

   G $\frac{15}{20}$

   H $\frac{3}{4}$

   J $\frac{2}{3}$

6. The average annual precipitation in Miami, FL is 57.55 inches. Express 57.55 as a mixed number.

   F $57\frac{11}{20}$

   G $57\frac{55}{1000}$

   H $57\frac{5}{100}$

   J $57\frac{1}{20}$

Three of the World's Smallest Nations

Nation	Area (square miles)
Vatican City	0.17
Monaco	0.75
Nauru	8.2

5. What is the area of Nauru expressed as a mixed number?

   A $8\frac{1}{50}$

   C $8\frac{2}{100}$

   B $8\frac{2}{50}$

   D $8\frac{1}{5}$

7. The average annual precipitation in Norfolk, VA is 45.22 inches. Express 45.22 as a mixed number.

   A $45\frac{11}{50}$

   C $45\frac{11}{20}$

   B $45\frac{22}{1000}$

   D $45\frac{1}{5}$

Holt McDougal Mathematics

LESSON 2 — Rational Numbers

Problem Solving: Multiplying Rational Numbers

Use the table at the right.

1. What was the average number of births per minute in 2001?

   _____

Average World Births and Deaths per Second in 2001

Births	$4\frac{1}{5}$
Deaths	1.7

2. What was the average number of deaths per hour in 2001?

   _____

3. What was the average number of births per day in 2001?

   _____

4. What was the average number of births in $\frac{1}{2}$ of a second in 2001?

   _____

5. What was the average number of births in $\frac{1}{4}$ of a second in 2001?

   _____

Use the table below. During exercise, the target heart rate is 0.5–0.75 of the maximum heart rate. Choose the letter for the best answer.

6. What is the target heart rate range for a 14 year old?

   A 7–10.5

   B 103–154.5

   C 145–166

   D 206–255

Age	Maximum Heart Rate
13	207
14	206
15	205
20	200
25	195

Source: American Heart Association

7. What is the target heart rate range for a 20 year old?

   F 100–150

   G 125–175

   H 150–200

   J 200–250

8. What is the target heart rate range for a 25 year old?

   A 25–75

   B 85–125

   C 97.5–146.25

   D 195–250

LESSON 3 Rational Numbers

Problem Solving: Dividing Rational Numbers

Use the table at the right that shows the maximum speed over a quarter mile of different animals. Find the time it takes each animal to travel one-quarter mile at top speed. Round to the nearest thousandth.

1. Quarter horse

   _____

2. Greyhound

   _____

3. Human

   _____

4. Giant tortoise

   _____

Maximum Speeds of Animals

Animal	Speed (mph)
Quarter horse	47.50
Greyhound	39.35
Human	27.89
Giant tortoise	0.17
Three-toed sloth	0.15

5. Three-toed sloth

   _____

Choose the letter for the best answer.

6. A piece of ribbon is $1\frac{7}{8}$ inches long. If the ribbon is going to be divided into 15 pieces, how long should each piece be?

   A $\frac{1}{8}$ in.　　　C $\frac{2}{3}$ in.

   B $\frac{1}{15}$ in.　　　D $28\frac{1}{8}$ in.

7. The recorded rainfall for each day of a week was 0 in., $\frac{1}{4}$ in., $\frac{3}{4}$ in., 1 in., 0 in., $1\frac{1}{4}$ in., $1\frac{1}{4}$ in. What was the average rainfall per day?

   F $\frac{9}{10}$ in.　　　H $\frac{7}{8}$ in.

   G $\frac{9}{14}$ in.　　　J $4\frac{1}{2}$ in.

8. A drill bit that is $\frac{7}{32}$ in. means that the hole the bit makes has a diameter of $\frac{7}{32}$ in. Since the radius is half of the diameter, what is the radius of a hole drilled by a $\frac{7}{32}$ in. bit?

   A $\frac{14}{32}$ in.　　　C $\frac{9}{16}$ in.

   B $\frac{7}{32}$ in.　　　D $\frac{7}{64}$ in.

9. A serving of a certain kind of cereal is $\frac{2}{3}$ cup. There are 12 cups of cereal in the box. How many servings of cereal are in the box?

   F 18

   G 15

   H 8

   J 6

Name _____ Date _____ Class_____

LESSON 4

Rational Numbers
Problem Solving: Adding and Subtracting with Unlike Denominators

Write the correct answer.

1. Nick Hysong of the United States won the Olympic gold medal in the pole vault in 2000 with a jump of 19 ft $4\frac{1}{4}$ inches, or $232\frac{1}{4}$ inches. In 1900, Irving Baxter of the United States won the pole vault with a jump of 10 ft $9\frac{7}{8}$ inches, or $129\frac{7}{8}$ inches. How much higher did Hysong vault than Baxter?

_____

2. In the 2000 Summer Olympics, Ivan Pedroso of Cuba won the Long jump with a jump of 28 ft $\frac{3}{4}$ inches, or $336\frac{3}{4}$ inches. Alvin Kraenzlein of the United States won the long jump in 1900 with a jump of 23 ft $6\frac{7}{8}$ inches, or $282\frac{7}{8}$ inches. How much farther did Pedroso jump than Kraenzlein?

_____

3. A recipe calls for $\frac{1}{8}$ cup of sugar and $\frac{3}{4}$ cup of brown sugar. How much total sugar is added to the recipe?

4. The average snowfall in Norfolk, VA for January is $2\frac{3}{5}$ inches, February $2\frac{9}{10}$ inches, March 1 inch, and December $\frac{9}{10}$ inches. If these are the only months it typically snows, what is the average snowfall per year?

_____

Use the table at the right that shows the average snowfall per month in Vail, Colorado.

5. What is the average annual snowfall in Vail, Colorado?

   A $15\frac{13}{20}$ in.   C $187\frac{1}{10}$ in.

   B 153 in.   D $187\frac{4}{5}$ in.

6. The peak of the skiing season is from December through March. What is the average snowfall for this period?

   F $30\frac{19}{20}$ in.   H $123\frac{4}{5}$ in.

   G $123\frac{3}{5}$ in.   J 127 in.

Average Snowfall in Vail, CO

Month	Snowfall (in.)	Month	Snowfall (in.)
Jan	$36\frac{7}{10}$	July	0
Feb	$35\frac{7}{10}$	August	0
March	$25\frac{2}{5}$	Sept	1
April	$21\frac{1}{5}$	Oct	$7\frac{4}{5}$
May	4	Nov	$29\frac{7}{10}$
June	$\frac{3}{10}$	Dec	26

Holt McDougal Mathematics

Rational Numbers

Problem Solving: Solving Equations with Rational Numbers

Write the correct answer.

1. In the last 150 years, the average height of people in industrialized nations has increased by $\frac{1}{3}$ foot. Today, American men have an average height of $5\frac{7}{12}$ feet. What was the average height of American men 150 years ago?

2. Jaime has a length of ribbon that is $23\frac{1}{2}$ in. long. If she plans to cut the ribbon into pieces that are $\frac{3}{4}$ in. long, into how many pieces can she cut the ribbon? (She cannot use partial pieces.)

3. Todd's restaurant bill for dinner was $15.55. After he left a tip, he spent a total of $18.00 on dinner. How much money did Todd leave for a tip?

4. The difference between the boiling point and melting point of Hydrogen is 6.47 °C. The melting point of Hydrogen is −259.34 °C. What is the boiling point of Hydrogen?

Choose the letter for the best answer.

5. In 2005, a sprinter won the gold medal in the 100-m dash in with a time of 9.85 seconds. His time was 0.95 seconds faster than the winner in the 100-m dash in 1900. What was winner's time in 1900?

   A 8.95 seconds

   B 10.65 seconds

   C 10.80 seconds

   D 11.20 seconds

7. After a morning shower, there was $\frac{17}{100}$ in. of rain in the rain gauge. It rained again an hour later and the rain gauge showed $\frac{1}{4}$ in. of rain. How much did it rain the second time?

   A $\frac{2}{25}$ in.   C $\frac{21}{50}$ in.

   B $\frac{1}{6}$ in.   D $\frac{3}{8}$ in.

6. The balance in Susan's checking account was $245.35. After the bank deposited interest into the account, her balance went to $248.02. How much interest did the bank pay Susan?

   F $1.01

   G $2.67

   H $3.95

   J $493.37

8. Two-third of John's savings account is being saved for his college education. If $2500 of his savings is for his college education, how much money in total is in his savings account?

   F $1666.67   H $4250.83

   G $3750   J $5000

LESSON 6 Rational Numbers

Problem Solving: Solving Two-Step Equations

The chart below describes three different long-distance calling plans. Jamie has budgeted $20 per month for long-distance calls. Write the correct answer.

1. How many minutes will Jamie be able to use per month with plan A? Round to the nearest minute.

_____

Plan	Monthly Access Fee	Charge per minute
A	$3.95	$0.08
B	$8.95	$0.06
C	$0	$0.10

2. How many minutes will Jamie be able to use per month with plan B? Round to the nearest minute.

3. How many minutes will Jamie be able to use per month with plan C? Round to the nearest minute.

_____

4. Which plan is the best deal for Jamie's budget?

5. Nolan has budgeted $50 per month for long distance. Which plan is the best deal for Nolan's budget?

_____

The table describes four different car loans that Susana can get to finance her new car. The total column gives the amount she will end up paying for the car including the down payment and the payments with interest. Choose the letter for the best answer.

6. How much will Susana pay each month with loan A?

  A $252.04   C $330.35

  B $297.02   D $353.68

7. How much will Susana pay each month with loan B?

  F $300.85   H $323.17

  G $306.50   J $383.14

8. How much will Susana pay each month with loan C?

  A $336.62   C $369.95

  B $352.28   D $420.78

Loan	Down Payment	Number of Months	Total
A	$2000	60	$19,821.20
B	$1000	48	$19,390.72
C	$0	60	$20,197.20

9. Which loan will give Susana the smallest monthly payment?

  F Loan A   H Loan C

  G Loan B   J They are equal

Graphs and Functions

Problem Solving: Ordered Pairs

Use the table at the right for Exercises 1–2.

1. Write the ordered pair that shows the average miles per gallon in 1990.

   _____

2. The data can be approximated by the equation $m = 0.30887x - 595$ where m is the average miles per gallon and x is the year. Use the equation to find an ordered pair (x, m) that shows the estimated miles per gallon in the year 2020.

   _____

Average Miles per Gallon

Year	Miles per Gallon
1970	13.5
1980	15.9
1990	20.2
1995	21.1
1996	21.2
1997	21.5

For Exercises 3–4 use the equation $F = 1.8C + 32$, which relates Fahrenheit temperatures F to Celsius temperatures C.

3. Write ordered pair (C, F) that shows the Celsius equivalent of 86 °F.

   _____

4. Write ordered pair (C, F) that shows the Fahrenheit equivalent of 22 °C.

   _____

Choose the letter for the best answer.

5. A taxi charges a $2.50 flat fee plus $0.30 per mile. Use an equation for taxi fare t in terms of miles m. Which ordered pair (m, t) shows the taxi fare for a 23-mile cab ride?

   A (23, 6.90)   C (23, 9.40)

   B (23, 18.50)   D (23, 64.40)

6. The perimeter p of a square is four times the length of a side s, or $p = 4s$. Which ordered pair (s, p) shows the perimeter for a square that has sides that are 5 in.?

   F (5, 1.25)   H (5, 9)

   G (5, 20)   J (5, 25)

7. Maria pays a monthly fee of $3.95 plus $0.10 per minute for long-distance calls. Use an equation for the phone bill p in terms of the number of minutes m. Which ordered pair (m, p) shows the phone bill for 120 minutes?

   A (120, 15.95)   C (120, 28.30)

   B (120, 474.10)   D (120, 486.00)

8. Tickets to a baseball game cost $12 each, plus $2 each for transportation. Use an equation for the cost c of going to the game in terms of the number of people p. Which ordered pair (p, c) shows the cost for 6 people?

   F (6, 74)   H (6, 84)

   G (6, 96)   J (6, 102)

LESSON 2 Graphs and Functions

Problem Solving: Graphing on the Coordinate Plane

Graph the points to answer each question.

1. Graph the points (–4, 1), (–4, –2), (1, 1), and (1, –2).

2. What type of quadrilateral do the vertices form?

   _____

3. What is the perimeter of the figure?

   _____

4. What is the area of the figure?

   _____

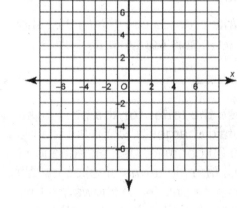

5. Graph the points (–3, 1), (–3, –5), (3, 1), and (3, –5).

6. What type of polygon do the vertices form?

   _____

7. What is the perimeter of the figure?

   _____

8. What is the area of the figure?

   _____

Solve each problem.

9. The point (4, –2) is in which quadrant?

   A I   C III

   B II   D IV ⟲

10. The point (–1, 7) is in which quadrant?

    A I   C III

    B II ⟲   D IV

11. Which of the following points is the same distance from (–2, 3) as (3, 3)?

    A (3, –2)   C (3, 8)

    B (–2, –2)   D (–1, 3)

12. A rectangle is formed with the vertices (0, 0), (6, 0), and (0, 5). Which point is the fourth vertex of the rectangle?

    A (–6, 5)   C (6, 5)

    B (5, 5)   D (0, –5)

LESSON 3 — Graphs and Functions

Problem Solving: Interpreting Graphs

Tell which table corresponds to each situation.

1. Ryan walks for several blocks, and then he begins to run. After running for 10 minutes, he walks for several blocks and then stops.

   Table 2

2. Susanna starts running. After 10 minutes, she sees a friend and stops to talk. When she leaves her friend, she runs home and stops.

   Table 3

3. Mark stands on the porch and talks to a friend. Then he starts walking home. Part way home he decides to run the rest of the way, and he doesn't stop until he gets home.

   Table 1

Table 1

Time	Speed (mi/h)
8:00	0
8:10	3
8:20	7.5
8:30	0

Table 2

Time	Speed (mi/h)
8:00	3
8:10	7.5
8:20	3
8:30	0

Table 3

Time	Speed (mi/h)
8:00	7.5
8:10	0
8:20	7.5
8:30	0

The graph represents the height of water in a bathtub over time. Choose the correct letter.

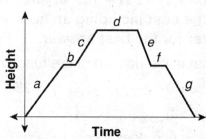

4. Which part of the graph best represents the tub being filled with water?

   A a   C c
   B d   D g

5. Which part of the graph shows the tub being drained of water?

   A c   C d
   B e   D g

7. Which part of the graph shows when someone gets into the tub?

   A a   C c
   B e   D f

6. Which part of the graph shows someone soaking in the tub?

   F b   H d
   G e   J f

8. Which parts of the graph show when the water level is not changing in the tub?

   F a, b, c   H b, d, g
   G b, d, f   J c, e, f

Name _____ Date _____ Class_____

Graphs and Functions

Problem Solving: Functions

A cyclist rides at an average speed of 20 miles per hour. The equation $y = 20x$ shows the distance, y, the cyclist travels in x hours.

1. Make a table for the equation and graph the equation at the right.

x	20x	y
0	20(0)	0
1	20(1)	20
2	20(2)	40
3	20(3)	60

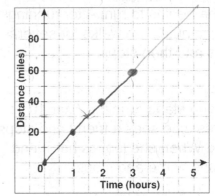

2. Is the relationship between the time and the distance the cyclist rides a function?

Yes

3. If the cyclist continues to ride at the same rate, about how far will the cyclist ride in 4 hours?

80 mi

4. About how far does the cyclist ride in 1.5 hours?

30 mi

5. If the cyclist has ridden 50 miles, about how long has the cyclist been riding?

2.5 hrs.

The cost of renting a jet-ski at a lake is represented by the equation $f(x) = 25x + 100$ where x is the number of hours and $f(x)$ is the cost including an hourly rate and a deposit. Choose the letter for the best answer.

6. What is the domain of the function?

   A $x < 0$ C $x > 25$

   B $x > 0$ D $x < 100$

7. What is the range of the function?

   F $f(x) > 0$ H $f(x) < 25$

   G $f(x) < 0$ J $f(x) > 100$

8. How much does it cost to rent the jet-ski for 5 hours?

   A $125   C $385

   B $225   D $525

9. If the cost to rent the jet-ski is $300, for how many hours is the jet-ski rented?

   F 6 hours   H 12 hours

   G 8 hours   J 16 hours

LESSON 5 Graphs and Functions

Problem Solving: Equations, Tables, and Graphs

Use the graph to answer Exercises 1–4. An aquarium tank is being drained. The graph shows the number of gallons of water, q, in the tank after m minutes. Write the correct answer.

1. How many gallons of water are in the tank before it is drained?

   _____

2. How many gallons of water are left in the tank after 2 minutes?

   _____

3. How long does it take until there are 10 gallons of water left in the tank?

   _____

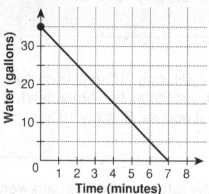

4. How long does it take to drain the tank?

   _____

Use the graph to answer Exercises 5–7. The graph shows the distance, d, a hiker can hike in h hours. Choose the letter of the best answer.

5. How far can the hiker hike in 4 hours?

   A $1\frac{1}{3}$ mi   C 8 mi

   B 4 mi   D 12 mi

6. How long does it take the hiker to hike 6 miles?

   F $2h$ H $4h$

   G $3h$ J $18h$

7. Which equation represents the graph?

   A $d = 3h$ C $d = h + 3$

   B $d = \frac{1}{3}h$ D $d = h - 3$

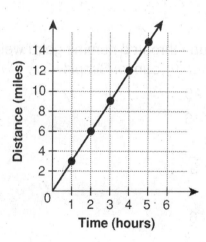

LESSON 1 Exponents and Roots
Problem Solving: Integer Exponents

Write the correct answer.

1. The weight of 10^7 dust particles is 1 gram. Simplify 10^7.

   _____

2. The weight of one dust particle is 10^{-7} gram. Simplify 10^{-7}.

   _____

3. As of 2001, only 10^6 rural homes in the United States had broadband Internet access. Simplify 10^6.

   _____

4. Atomic clocks measure time in microseconds. A microsecond is 10^{-6} second. Simplify 10^{-6}.

   _____

Choose the letter for the best answer.

5. The diameter of the nucleus of an atom is about 10^{-15} meter. Simplify 10^{-15}.

   A 0.0000000000001

   B 0.00000000000001

   C 0.0000000000000001

   D 0.000000000000001

6. The diameter of the nucleus of an atom is 0.000001 nanometer. How many nanometers is the diameter of the nucleus of an atom?

   F $(-10)^5$

   G $(-10)^6$

   H 10^{-6}

   J 10^{-5}

7. A ruby-throated hummingbird weighs about 3^{-2} ounce. Simplify 3^{-2}.

   A −9

   B −6

   C $\dfrac{1}{9}$

   D $\dfrac{1}{6}$

8. A ruby-throated hummingbird breathes 2×5^3 times per minute while at rest. Simplify this amount.

   F 1,000

   G 250

   H 125

   J 30

LESSON 2

Exponents and Roots

Problem Solving: Properties of Exponents

Write each answer as a power.

1. Cindy separated her fruit flies into equal groups. She estimates that there are 2^{10} fruit flies in each of 2^2 jars. How many fruit flies does Cindy have in all?

_____

2. Suppose a researcher tests a new method of pasteurization on a strain of bacteria in his laboratory. If the bacteria are killed at a rate of 8^9 per sec, how many bacteria would be killed after 8^2 sec?

_____

3. A satellite orbits the earth at about 13^4 km per hour. How long would it take to complete 24 orbits, which is a distance of about 13^5 km?

_____

4. The side of a cube is 3^4 centimeters long. What is the volume of the cube? (Hint: $V = s^3$.)

_____

Use the table to answer Exercises 5–6. The table describes the number of people involved at each level of a pyramid scheme. In a pyramid scheme each individual recruits so many others to participate who in turn recruit others, and so on. Choose the letter of the best answer.

5. Using exponents, how many people will be involved at level 6?

   A 6^6 C 5^5

   B 6^5 D 5^6

6. How many times as many people will be involved at level 6 than at level 2?

   F 5^4 H 5^5

   G 5^3 J 5^6

7. There are 10^3 ways to make a 3-digit combination, but there are 10^6 ways to make a 6-digit combination. How many times more ways are there to make a 6-digit combination than a 3-digit combination?

   A 5^{10} C 2^5

   B 2^{10} D 10^3

Pyramid Scheme
Each person recruits 5 others.

Level	Total Number of People
1	5
2	5^2
3	5^3
4	5^4

8. After 3 hours, a bacteria colony has $(25^3)^3$ bacteria present. How many bacteria are in the colony?

   F 25^1 H 25^9

   G 25^6 J 25^{33}

LESSON
3

Exponents and Roots

Problem Solving: Scientific Notation

Write the correct answer.

1. In June 2001, the Intel Corporation announced that they could produce a silicon transistor that could switch on and off 1.5 trillion times a second. Express the speed of the transistor in scientific notation.

_____

2. With this transistor, computers will be able to do 1×10^9 calculations in the time it takes to blink your eye. Express the number of calculations using standard notation.

_____

3. The elements in this fast transistor are 20 nanometers long. A nanometer is one-billionth of a meter. Express the length of an element in the transistor in meters using scientific notation.

_____

4. The length of the elements in the transistor can also be compared to the width of a human hair. The length of an element is 2×10^{-3} times smaller than the width of a human hair. Express 2×10^{-3} in standard notation.

_____

Use the table to answer Exercises 5–9. Choose the best answer.

5. Express a light-year in miles using scientific notation.

   A 58.8×10^{11} C 588×10^{10}

   B 5.88×10^{12} D 5.88×10^{-13}

6. How many miles is it from Earth to the star Sirius?

   F 4.705×10^{12} H 7.35×10^{12}

   G 4.704×10^{13} J 7.35×10^{11}

7. How many miles is it from Earth to the star Canopus?

   A 3.822×10^{15} C 3.822×10^{14}

   B 1.230×10^{15} D 1.230×10^{14}

8. How many miles is it from Earth to the star Alpha Centauri?

   F 2.352×10^{13} H 2.352×10^{14}

   G 5.92×10^{13} J 5.92×10^{14}

Distance From Earth To Stars
Light-Year = 5,880,000,000,000 mi.

Star	Constellation	Distance (light-years)
Sirius	Canis Major	8
Canopus	Carina	650
Alpha Centauri	Centaurus	4
Vega	Lyra	23

9. How many miles is it from Earth to the star Vega?

   A 6.11×10^{13} C 6.11×10^{14}

   B 1.3524×10^{13} D 1.3524×10^{14}

Exponents and Roots

LESSON 4

Problem Solving: Operating with Scientific Notation

Write your answer in scientific notation.

1. The top speed of a garden snail is 3.0×10^{-2} miles per hour. The top speed of a cheetah is 7.0×10^1. How many times greater is the speed of the cheetah than the garden snail?

_____

2. The speed of light is approximately 1.86×10^5 miles per second. How many miles will light travel in a 24-hour day?

_____

3. The total area for the 50 U.S. states and Washington, D.C. is 3.79×10^6 square miles. Of that, 2.57×10^5 square miles are water. The rest of the area is land. How many square miles is the land area?

_____

4. In 2008, Americans spent $\$3.8 \times 10^9$ on bottled water and $\$2.7 \times 10^8$ on coffee. How much did Americans spend altogether on bottled water and coffee?

_____

Choose the letter for the best answer.

5. The all-time top grossing U.S. movie, *Titanic*, made $\$6.008 \times 10^8$. In 2008, *Dark Knight* was the top grossing movie at $\$5.309 \times 10^8$. How much did Titanic and Dark Knight gross in all?

   A $\$1.13 \times 10^9$

   B $\$3.19 \times 10^8$

   C $\$6.99 \times 10^8$

   D $\$8.84 \times 10^9$

6. A large department store chain employs 1.8×10^6 people. The average annual wage for the employees is $\$2.1 \times 10^4$. How much does the chain pay in employee wages each year?

   F $\$3.00 \times 10^2$

   G $\$3.78 \times 10^{10}$

   H $\$3.90 \times 10^{24}$

   J $\$8.57 \times 10^{10}$

7. Gary measures a paramecium and an ant. The paramecium is 4.2×10^{-4} meter long, and the ant is 3.8×10^{-3} meter long. How much longer, in meters, is the ant than the paramecium?

   A 4.00×10^{-2} C 3.82×10^{-3}

   B 3.38×10^{-3} D 4.22×10^{-3}

8. The average radius of Jupiter is 4.34×10^4 miles. The average radius of the Sun is 4.32×10^5. How many times greater is the average radius of the sun?

   F 1.00×10^1

   G 2.00×10^3

   H 4.75×10^1

   J 9.95×10^0

LESSON **5**

Exponents and Roots

Problem Solving: Squares and Square Roots

Write the correct answer.

1. For college wrestling competitions, the NCAA requires that the wrestling mat be a square with an area of 1764 square feet. What is the length of each side of the wrestling mat?

_____

2. For high school wrestling competitions, the wrestling mat must be a square with an area of 1444 square feet. What is the length of each side of the wrestling mat?

_____

3. The Japanese art of origami requires folding square pieces of paper. Elena begins with a large sheet of square paper that is 169 square inches. How many squares can she cut out of the paper that are 4 inches on each side?

_____

4. When the James family moved into a new house they had a square area rug that was 132 square feet. In their new house, there are three bedrooms. Bedroom one is 11 feet by 11 feet. Bedroom two is 10 feet by 12 feet and bedroom three is 13 feet by 13 feet. In which bedroom will the rug fit?

_____

Choose the letter for the best answer.

5. A square picture frame measures 36 inches on each side. The actual wood trim is 2 inches wide. The photograph in the frame is surrounded by a bronze mat that measures 5 inches. What is the maximum area of the photograph?

 A 841 sq. inches

 B 900 sq. inches

 C 1156 sq. inches

 D 484 sq. inches

6. To create a square patchwork quilt wall hanging, square pieces of material are sewn together to form a larger square. Which number of smaller squares can be used to create a square patchwork quilt wall hanging?

 F 35 squares   H 84 squares

 G 64 squares   J 125 squares

7. A can of paint claims that one can will cover 400 square feet. If you painted a square with the can of paint, how long would it be on each side?

 A 200 feet   C 25 feet

 B 65 feet   D 20 feet

8. A box of tile contains 12 square tiles. If you tile the largest possible square area using whole tiles, how many tiles will you have left from the box?

 F 9   H 3

 G 6   J 0

© Houghton Mifflin Harcourt Publishing Company

LESSON 6

Exponents and Roots

Problem Solving: Estimating Square Roots

The distance to the horizon can be found using the formula
$d = 112.88 \sqrt{h}$ **where** *d* **is the distance in kilometers and** *h* **is the number of kilometers from the ground. Round your answer to the nearest kilometer.**

1. How far is it to the horizon when you are standing on the top of Mt. Everest, a height of 8.85 km?

2. Find the distance to the horizon from the top of Mt. McKinley, Alaska, a height of 6.194 km.

_____

3. How far is it to the horizon if you are standing on the ground and your eyes are 2 m above the ground?

4. Mauna Kea is an extinct volcano on Hawaii that is about 4 km tall. You should be able to see the top of Mauna Kea when you are how far away?

_____

You can find the approximate speed of a vehicle that leaves skid marks before it stops. The formulas $S = 5.5\sqrt{0.7L}$ **and** $S = 5.5\sqrt{0.8L}$ **, where** *S* **is the speed in miles per hour and** *L* **is the length of the skid marks in feet, will give the minimum and maximum speeds that the vehicle was traveling before the brakes were applied. Round to the nearest mile per hour.**

5. A vehicle leaves a skid mark of 40 feet before stopping. What was the approximate speed of the vehicle before it stopped?

   A 25–35 mi/h   C 29–31 mi/h

   B 28–32 mi/h   D 68–70 mi/h

6. A vehicle leaves a skid mark of 100 feet before stopping. What was the approximate speed of the vehicle before it stopped?

   F 46–49 mi/h   H 62–64 mi/h

   G 50–55 mi/h   J 70–73 mi/h

7. A vehicle leaves a skid mark of 150 feet before stopping. What was the approximate speed of the vehicle before it stopped?

   A 50–55 mi/h   C 55–70 mi/h

   B 53–58 mi/h   D 56–60 mi/h

8. A vehicle leaves a skid mark of 200 feet before stopping. What was the approximate speed of the vehicle before it stopped?

   F 60–63 mi/h   H 72–78 mi/h

   G 65–70 mi/h   J 80–90 mi/h

    Holt McDougal Mathematics

Exponents and Roots

LESSON 7

Problem Solving: The Real Numbers

Write the correct answer.

1. Twin primes are prime numbers that differ by 2. Find an irrational number between twin primes 5 and 7.

2. Rounded to the nearest ten-thousandth, $\pi = 3.1416$. Find a rational number between 3 and π.

3. One famous irrational number is e. Rounded to the nearest ten-thousandth $e \approx 2.7183$. Find a rational number that is between 2 and e.

4. Perfect numbers are those for which the divisors of the number sum to the number itself. The number 6 is a perfect number because $1 + 2 + 3 = 6$. The number 28 is also a perfect number. Find an irrational number between 6 and 28.

Choose the letter for the best answer.

5. Which is a rational number?

   A the length of a side of a square with area 2 cm^2

   B the length of a side of a square with area 4 cm^2

   C a non-terminating decimal

   D the square root of a prime number

6. Which is an irrational number?

   F a number that can be expressed as a fraction

   G the length of a side of a square with area 4 cm^2

   H the length of a side of a square with area 2 cm^2

   J the square root of a negative number

7. Which is an integer?

   A the number half-way between 6 and 7

   B the average rainfall for the week if it rained 0.5 in., 2.3 in., 0 in., 0 in., 0 in., 0.2 in., 0.75 in. during the week

   C the money in an account if the balance was $213.00 and $21.87 was deposited

   D the net yardage after plays that resulted in a 15 yard loss, 10 yard gain, 6 yard gain and 5 yard loss

8. Which is a whole number?

   F the number half-way between 6 and 7

   G the total amount of sugar in a recipe that calls for $\frac{1}{4}$ cup of brown sugar and $\frac{3}{4}$ cup of granulated sugar

   H the money in an account if the balance was $213.00 and $21.87 was deposited

   J the net yardage after plays that resulted in a 15 yard loss, 10 yard gain, 6 yard gain and 5 yard loss

Holt McDougal Mathematics

Name _____ Date _____ Class_____

LESSON
8

Exponents and Roots

Problem Solving: The Pythagorean Theorem

Write the correct answer. Round to the nearest tenth.

1. A utility pole 10 m high is supported by two guy wires. Each guy wire is anchored 3 m from the base of the pole. How many meters of wire are needed for the guy wires?

2. A 12 foot-ladder is resting against a wall. The base of the ladder is 2.5 feet from the base of the wall. How high up the wall will the ladder reach?

3. The base-path of a baseball diamond form a square. If it is 90 ft from home to first, how far does the catcher have to throw to catch someone stealing second base?

4. A football field is 100 yards with 10 yards at each end for the end zones. The field is 45 yards wide. Find the length of the diagonal of the entire field, including the end zones.

Choose the letter for the best answer.

5. The frame of a kite is made from two strips of wood, one 27 inches long, and one 18 inches long. What is the perimeter of the kite? Round to the nearest tenth.

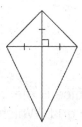

  A 18.8 in.   C 65.7 in.
  B 32.8 in.   D 131.2 in.

6. The glass for a picture window is 8 feet wide. The door it must pass through is 3 feet wide. How tall must the door be for the glass to pass through the door? Round to the nearest tenth.

  F 3.3 ft   H 7.4 ft
  G 6.7 ft   J 8.5 ft

7. A television screen measures approximately 15.5 in. high and 19.5 in. wide. A television is advertised by giving the approximate length of the diagonal of its screen. How should this television be advertised?

  A 25 in.   C 12 in.
  B 21 in.   D 6 in.

8. To meet federal guidelines, a wheelchair ramp that is constructed to rise 1 foot off the ground must extend 12 feet along the ground. How long will the ramp be? Round to the nearest tenth.

  F 11.9 ft   H 13.2 ft
  G 12.0 ft   J 15.0 ft

© Houghton Mifflin Harcourt Publishing Company

Holt McDougal Mathematics

Name _____ Date _____ Class_____

Exponents and Roots

9 **Problem Solving: Applying the Pythagorean Theorem and its Converse**

Solve each problem.

1. Linda made triangular flags for the spirit club to wave. Each flag was a right triangle. One side was 1.5 feet long and another side was 2.2 feet long. She used fringed trim along the longest side of the each flag. What was the length of fringed trim that she sewed to each flag? Round to the nearest tenth of a foot.

   _____

2. A wheelchair ramp starts 8 meters from the base of a staircase. The staircase is 1 meter high. What is the length of the wheelchair ramp? Round to the nearest tenth of a meter.

   _____

3. The city of Chicago is located at (4, 8) on a grid. The city of Memphis is located at (6, –12) on the grid. How many units apart are Chicago and Memphis on the grid? Round to the nearest tenth of a unit.

   _____

4. Tony needs to use a ladder to get onto the roof. The height of the house is about 11 feet. The ladder will be placed 6 feet from the house. What is the minimum height, to the nearest foot, that the ladder can be to safely reach the roof of the house?

   _____

Solve each problem.

5. An airplane is 33 miles due south and 56 miles due west of its destination airport. How far is the plane from the destination airport?

   A 9.4 miles   C 65 miles

   B 89 miles   D 4,225 miles

6. The location of a post office is marked at (2, 2) on a coordinate grid. Which point is about 18 units from the location of the post office?

   F L(–12, 9)   H M(12, 9)

   G N(12, –9)   J P(–12, –9)

7. A rectangular tabletop has a length of 3.3 feet and a width of 8.8 feet. Which is the length of its diagonal to the nearest tenth?

   A 88.33   C 29.04

   B 9.4   D 3.5

8. The location of three ships are shown on a coordinate grid by the following points: X(0, 7), Y(–5, –3), and Z(4, –1). Which ships are farthest apart?

   F X and Y   H X and Z

   G Y and Z   J Z and Y

© Houghton Mifflin Harcourt Publishing Company

Holt McDougal Mathematics

Name _____ Date _____ Class_____

Ratios, Proportions, and Similarity
Problem Solving: Ratios, Rates, and Unit Rates

Scientists have researched the ratio of brain weight to body size in different animals. The results are in the table below.

1. Order the animals by their brain weight to body weight ratio, from smallest to largest.

   _____

   _____

2. It has been hypothesized that the higher the brain weight to body weight ratio, the more intelligent the animal is. By this measure, which animals listed are the most intelligent?

   _____

3. Name two sets of animals that have approximately the same brain weight to body weight ratio.

   _____

Animal	Brain Weight / Body Weight
Cat	$\dfrac{1}{100}$
Dog	$\dfrac{1}{125}$
Elephant	$\dfrac{1}{560}$
Hippo	$\dfrac{1}{2789}$
Horse	$\dfrac{1}{600}$
Human	$\dfrac{1}{40}$
Small birds	$\dfrac{1}{12}$

Find the unit rate. Round to the nearest hundredth.

4. A 64-ounce bottle of apple juice costs $1.35.

   A $0.01/oz   C $0.47/oz

   B $0.02/oz   D $47.4/oz

5. Find the unit rate for a 2 lb package of hamburger that costs $3.45.

   F $0.58/lb   H $1.73/lb

   G $1.25/b   J $2.28/b

6. 12 slices of pizza cost $9.00.

   A $0.45/slice   C $0.75/slice

   B $0.50/slice   D $1.33/slice

7. John is selling 5 comic books for $6.00.

   F $0.83/book   H $1.02/book

   G $1.20/book   J $1.45/book

8. There are 64 beats in 4 measures of music.

   A 16 beats/measure

   B 12 beats/measure

   C 4 beats/measure

   D 0.06 beats/measure

9. The average price of a 30 second commercial for the 2002 Super Bowl was $1,900,000.

   F $120.82/sec

   G $1,242.50/sec

   H $5,839.02/sec

   J $63,333.33/sec

© Houghton Mifflin Harcourt Publishing Company

Holt McDougal Mathematics

LESSON 2

Ratios, Proportions, and Similarity
Problem Solving: Solving Proportions

Use the ratios in the table to answer each question. Round to the nearest tenth.

Body Part	$\dfrac{\text{Body Part}}{\text{Height}}$
Femur	$\dfrac{1}{4}$
Tibia	$\dfrac{1}{5}$
Hand span	$\dfrac{2}{17}$
Arm span	$\dfrac{1}{1}$
Head circumference	$\dfrac{1}{3}$

1. Which body part is the same length as the person's height?

   _____

2. If a person's tibia is 13 inches, how tall would you expect the person to be?

   _____

3. If a person's hand span is 8.5 inches, about how tall would you expect the person to be?

   _____

4. If a femur is 18 inches long, how many feet tall would you expect the person to be?

   _____

5. What would you expect the head circumference to be of a person who is 5.5 feet tall?

   _____

6. What would you expect the hand span to be of a person who is 5 feet tall?

   _____

Choose the letter for the best answer.

7. Five milliliters of a children's medicine contains 400 mg of the drug amoxicillin. How many mg of amoxicillin does 25 mL contain?

   A 0.3 mg   C 2000 mg

   B 80 mg   D 2500 mg

8. A basketball player for the Seattle Supersonics averages about 2 three-pointers for every 5 he shoots. If he attempts 10 three-pointers in a game, how many would you expect him to make?

   F 4   H 8

   G 5   J 25

9. In 2002, a 30-second commercial during the Super Bowl cost an average of $1,900,000. At this rate, how much would a 45-second commercial cost?

   A $1,266,666   C $3,500,000

   B $2,850,000   D $4,000,000

10. A medicine for dogs indicates that the medicine should be administered in the ratio 2 teaspoons per 5 lb, based on the weight of the dog. How much should be given to a 70 lb dog?

    F 5 teaspoons   H 14 teaspoons

    G 12 teaspoons   J 28 teaspoons

LESSON 3

Ratios, Proportions, and Similarity
Problem Solving: Similar Figures

Write the correct answer.

1. Until 1929, United States currency measured 3.13 in. by 7.42 in. The current size is 2.61 in. by 6.14 in. Are the bills similar?

2. Owen has a 3 in. by 5 in. photograph. He wants to make it as large as he can to fit in a 10 in. by 12.5 in. ad. What scale factor will he use? What will be the new size?

3. A painting is 15 cm long and 8 cm wide. In a reproduction that is similar to the original painting, the length is 36 cm. How wide is the reproduction?

4. The two shortest sides of a right triangle are 10 in. and 24 in. long. What is the length of the shortest side of a similar right triangle whose two longest sides are 36 in. and 39 in.?

The scale on a map is 1 inch = 40 miles. Round to the nearest mile.

5. On the map, it is 5.75 inches from Orlando to Miami. How many miles is it from Orlando to Miami?

   A 46 miles   C 230 miles

   B 175 miles   D 340 miles

6. On the map it is $18\frac{1}{8}$ inches from Norfolk, VA, to Indianapolis, IN. How many miles is it from Norfolk to Indianapolis?

   F 58 miles   H 800 miles

   G 725 miles   J 1025 miles

7. It is 185 miles from Chicago to Indianapolis. On the map it is 2.5 inches from Indianapolis to Terra Haute, IN. How far is it from Chicago to Terra Haute going through Indianapolis?

   A 100 miles   C 430 miles

   B 285 miles   D 7500 miles

8. On the map, it is 7.5 inches from Chicago to Cincinnati. Traveling at 65 mi/h, how long will it take to drive from Chicago to Cincinnati? Round to the nearest tenth of an hour.

   F 4.6 hours   H 8.7 hours

   G 5.2 hours   J 12.0 hours

LESSON 4

Ratios, Proportions, and Similarity
Problem Solving: Dilations

Write the correct answer.

1. When you enlarge something on a photocopy machine, is the image a dilation?

_____

2. When you make a photocopy that is the same size, is the image a dilation? If so, what is the scale factor?

_____

3. In the movie *Honey, I Blew Up the Kid,* a two-year-old-boy is enlarged to a height of 112 feet. If the average height of a two-year old boy is 3 feet, what is the scale factor of this enlargement?

_____

4. In the movie *Honey, I Shrunk the Kids,* an inventor shrinks his kids by a scale factor of about $\frac{1}{240}$. If his kids were about 5 feet tall, how many inches tall were they after they were shrunk?

_____

Use the coordinate plane for Exercises 5–6. Round to the nearest tenth. Choose the letter for the best answer.

5. What will be the coordinates of *A'*, *B'* and *C'* after △*ABC* is dilated by a factor of 5?

   A *A'* (5, 10), *B'* (7, 8), *C'* (3, 8)

   B *A'* (0, 25), *B'* (10, 15), *C'* (–10, 15)

   C *A'* (0, 5), *B'* (10, 3), *C'* (–10, 3)

   D *A'* (0, 15), *B'* (2, 15), *C'* (–2, 15)

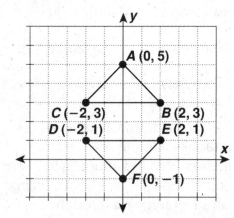

6. What will be the coordinates of *D'*, *E'* and *F'* after △*DEF* is dilated by a factor of 5?

   F *D'* (–10, 5), *E'* (10, 5), *F'* (0, –5)

   G *D'* (10, 5), *E'* (5, 5), *F'* (0, 5)

   H *D'* (10, 0), *E'* (5, 0), *F'* (–5, 0)

   J *D'* (10, 5), *E'* (5, 5), *F'* (–10, 0)

7. The projection of a movie onto a screen is a dilation. The universally accepted film size for movies has a width of 35 mm. If a movie screen is 12 m wide, what is the dilation factor?

   A 420   C 342.9

   B 0.3   D 2916.7

LESSON 1 — Geometric Relationships

Problem Solving: Angle Relationships

Use the flag of the Bahamas to solve the problems.

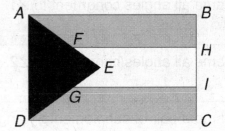

1. Name a right angle in the flag.

   _____

2. Name a pair of complementary angles in the flag.

   _____

3. Name two acute angles in the flag.

   _____

4. Name a pair of supplementary angles in the flag.

   _____

The diagram illustrates a ray of light being reflected off a mirror. The angle of incidence is congruent to the angle of reflection. Choose the letter for the best answer.

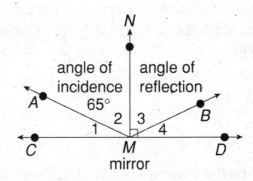

5. Name a pair of supplementary angles.

   A ∠CMA, ∠AMN,

   B ∠NMB, ∠AMB

   C ∠NMC, ∠DMN

   D ∠AMN, ∠NMD

6. Name a pair of complementary angles.

   F ∠NMB, ∠BMD

   G ∠AMN, ∠NMB

   H ∠CMA, ∠AMD

   J ∠CMA, ∠DMB

7. Which angle is congruent to ∠2?

   A ∠1   C ∠3

   B ∠4   D none

9. Find the measure of ∠1.

   A 65°   C 25°

   B 35°   D 90°

8. Find the measure of ∠4.

   F 65°   H 25°

   G 35°   J 90°

10. Find the measure of ∠3.

   F 90°   H 35°

   G 45°   J 65°

Holt McDougal Mathematics

LESSON	**Geometric Relationships**
2	**Problem Solving: Parallel and Perpendicular Lines**

The figure shows the layout of parking spaces in a parking lot.
$\overline{AB} \parallel \overline{CD} \parallel \overline{EF}$

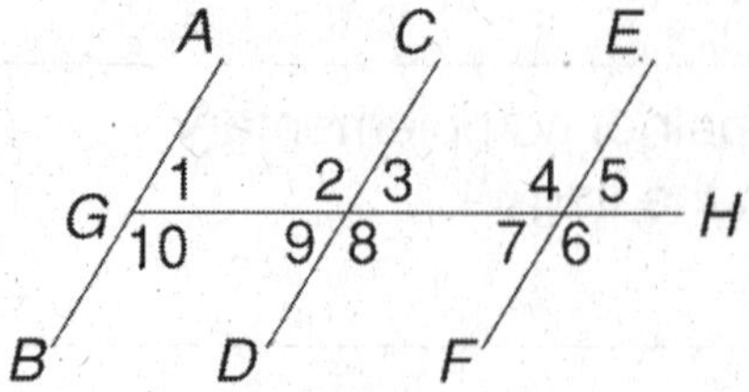

1. Name all angles congruent to ∠1.

   _____

2. Name all angles congruent to ∠2.

   _____

3. Name a pair of supplementary angles.

   _____

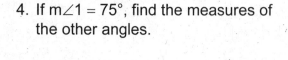

4. If m∠1 = 75°, find the measures of the other angles.

   _____

   _____

5. Name a pair of vertical angles.

   _____

6. If m∠1 = 90°, then $\overline{GH}$ is perpendicular to

   _____

The figure shows a board that will be cut along parallel segments GB and CF. $\overline{AD} \parallel \overline{HE}$. Choose the letter for the best answer.

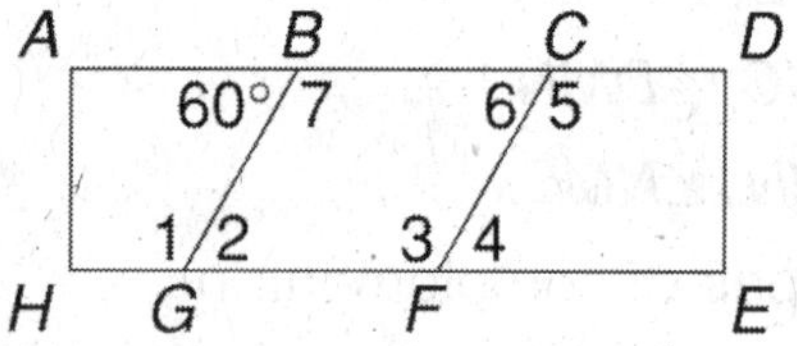

7. Find the measure of ∠1.

   A 45°   C 60°

   B 120°   D 90°

8. Find the measure of ∠2.

   F 30°   H 60°

   G 120°   J 90°

10. Find the measure of ∠4.

    F 45°   H 60°

    G 120°   J 90°

12. Find the measure of ∠6.

    F 30°   H 60°

    G 120°   J 90°

9. Find the measure of ∠3.

   A 30°   C 60°

   B 120°   D 90°

11. Find the measure of ∠5.

    A 30°   C 60°

    B 120°   D 90°

13. Find the measure of ∠7.

    A 45°   C 60°

    B 120°   D 90°

Name _____ Date _____ Class _____

LESSON
3 **Geometric Relationships**
Problem Solving: Triangles

The American flag must be folded according to certain rules
that result in the flag being folded into the shape of a triangle.
The figure shows a frame designed to hold an American flag.

1. Is the triangle acute, right, or obtuse?

_____

2. Is the triangle equilateral, isosceles,
   or scalene?

_____

3. Find $x°$.

_____

4. Find $y°$.

_____

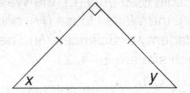

The figure shows a map of three streets. Choose the letter for
the best answer.

5. Find $x°$.

   A 22°   C 30°

   B 128°   D 68°

6. Find $w°$.

   F 22°   H 30°

   G 128°   J 52°

7. Find $y°$.

   A 22°

   B 30°

   C 128°

   D 143°

8. Find $z°$.

   F 22°

   G 30°

   H 128°

   J 143°

9. Which word best describes the
   triangle formed by the streets?

   A acute

   B right

   C obtuse

   D equilateral

10. Which word best describes the
    triangle formed by the streets?

    F equilateral

    G isosceles

    H scalene

    J acute

© Houghton Mifflin Harcourt Publishing Company

Holt McDougal Mathematics

Geometric Relationships
Problem Solving: Coordinate Geometry

Nguyen and his family went to Washington D.C. Nguyen graphed the sites he and his family visited on a coordinate grid.

1. On Saturday, Nguyen and his family visited the Lincoln Memorial (*L*), the Washington Monument (*W*), the White House (*H*), and the National Academy of Sciences (*N*) The coordinates for each site are *L*(–4, 2), *W*(2, 2), *H*(2, 6) and

   $N(-3, 3\frac{1}{2})$. Graph and label the coordinates.

   Connect the vertices. Give the most specific name for the polygon formed.

   _____

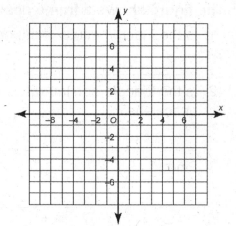

2. The White House, the Washington Memorial, and the Smithsonian form triangle

   HWS. Triangle *HWS* has a right angle at *W*. $\overline{WS}$ is $3\frac{1}{2}$ units. What are possible

   coordinates of the Smithsonian (*S*)? _____

3. The Department of the Interior is located at the midpoint of the White House and the Lincoln Memorial. What are the coordinates where the Department of the Interior is located? _____.

Choose the letter for the best answer.

4. A city map shows the State Capital at *C*(5, 3) and a Vietnam Veterans Memorial at *V*(–7, 3). Find the coordinates for the midpoint of the cities, *M*?

   A (1, 3)   C (–3, 1)

   B (3, 1)   D (–1, 3)

5. The location of four boats are shown on a coordinate grid. The boats are located at *S*(5, 3), *H*(5, 5) *I*(–7, 5), and *P*(–7, 3). What polygon is formed by the ships?

   F kite   H square

   G rectangle   J trapezoid

6. An architect is trying to draw an isosceles right triangle on a grid to use in his next blueprint. He has a point at (6, 3) and a point at (–2, 3). What could be the third point?

   A (–2, 0)   C (2, –2)

   B (6, –5)   D (6, 8)

7. Two points on an electrician's diagram are located at (5, 3) and (–7, 3). The scale on the diagram is 1 unit = 0.25 m. What is the actual distance between the two points?

   F 1 m   H 3 m

   G 2 m   J 4 m

Name ______________________ Date ______________ Class ______________

LESSON 5

Geometric Relationships

Problem Solving: Congruence

Use the American patchwork quilt block design called Carnival to answer the questions. Triangle *AIH* ≅ Triangle *AIB*, Triangle *ACJ* ≅ Triangle *AGJ*, Triangle *GFJ* ≅ Triangle *CDJ*.

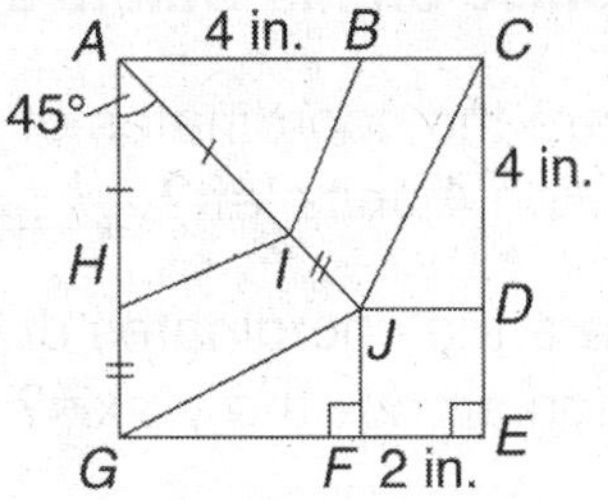

1. What is the measure of ∠*IAB*?

____

2. What is the measure of $\overline{AH}$?

____

3. What is the measure of $\overline{AG}$?

____

4. What is the measure of ∠*JDC*?

____

5. What is the measure of $\overline{FG}$?

____

The sketch is part of a bridge. Trapezoid *ABEF* ≅ Trapezoid *DEBC*. Choose the letter for the best answer.

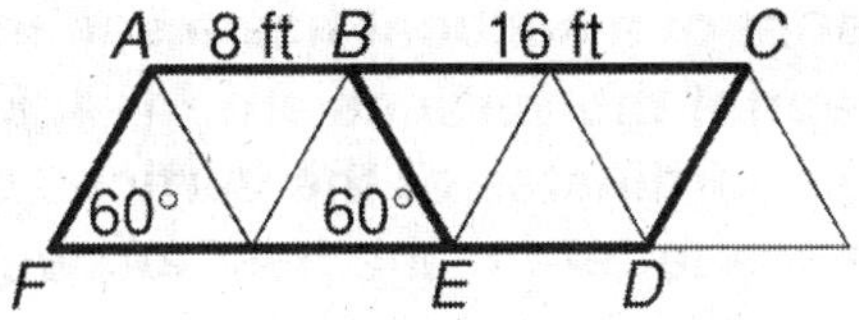

6. What is the measure of $\overline{DE}$?
   A 4 feet
   B 8 feet
   C 16 feet
   D Cannot be determined

7. What is the measure of $\overline{FE}$?
   F 4 feet H 8 feet
   G 16 feet J 24 feet

8. What is the measure of ∠*FAB*?
   A 45° C 60°
   B 90° D 120°

9. What is the measure of ∠*ABE*?
   F 45° H 60°
   G 90° J 120°

10. What is the measure of ∠*EBC*?
   A 45° C 60°
   B 90° D 120°

11. What is the measure of ∠*BED*?
   F 45° H 60°
   G 90° J 120°

12. What is the measure of ∠*BCD*?
   A 45° C 60°
   B 90° D 120°

Name _____ Date _____ Class _____

Geometric Relationships
Problem Solving: Transformations

Drew is going to hang a flag in his bedroom that is in the shape of a trapezoid. The grid below represents Drew's wall. The flag, a trapezoid ABCD, has vertices A(–1, –1), B(2, –1), C(4, –4), and D(–1, –4). Graph the transformations that Drew performs to find the right place on his wall to answer the questions.

1. What are the coordinates of Point *A* after a translation 4 units left? _____

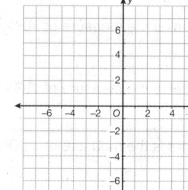

2. What are the coordinates of Point *B* after a reflection across the *y*-axis?

   _____

3. What are the coordinates of Point *C* after a 90° counterclockwise rotation around the origin?

   _____

4. What are the coordinates of Point *D* after a 180° clockwise rotation around the origin?

   _____

A blueprint of a sailboat has a sail in the shape of a right triangle, RST. On the blueprint the vertices are R(–4, 6), S(–4, 2) and T(1, 2). Use the rules to find the coordinates of the vertices of the sailboat as it changes position. Choose the letter for the best answer.

5. What are the coordinates of the sail after a reflection over the *x*-axis?

   A R(–4, 6), S(–4, 2), T(1, 2)

   B R(–4, –6), S(–4, –2), T(1, –2)

   C R(6, –4), S(2, –4), T(2, 1)

   D R(–6, –4), S(–2, –4), T(2, 1)

6. What are the coordinates of the sail after a translation left 3 units and a reflection over the *y*-axis?

   F R(7, 6), S(7, 2), T(2, 2)

   G R(7, –6), S(7, –2), T(2, –2)

   H R(–7, –6), S(–7, –2), T(–2, –2)

   J R(–6, –7), S(–2, –7), T(–2, –2)

7. What are the coordinates of Point *R* after a translation 1 unit left and a 90° clockwise rotation about (0, 0)?

   A R(5, 6)   C R(–5, 6)

   B R(–6, –5)   D R(6, 5)

8. What are the coordinates of Point *S* after a translation 4 units to the right and 5 units down?

   F S(–3, 0)   H S(0, 3)

   G S(0, –3)   J S(3, 0)

Name _____ Date _____ Class_____

LESSON 7 Geometric Relationships

Problem Solving: Similarity and Congruence Transformations

Identify each transformation and tell whether the two figures are similar or congruent.

1. Original: $A(-5, 6)$, $B(3, 6)$, $C(-3, 2)$
   Image: $A'(5, 6)$, $B'(-3, 6)$, $C'(3, 2)$

   _____

   _____

2. Original: $A(4, -2)$, $B(7, -1)$, $C(4, -7)$
   Image: $A'(1, 1)$, $B'(4, 2)$, $C'(1, -4)$

   _____

   _____

3. Original: $A(-3, -3)$, $B(0, 0)$, $C(3, -3)$,
   $D(0, -5)$
   Image: $A'(-4.5, -4.5)$, $B'(0, 0)$,
   $C'(4.5, -4.5)$, $D'(0, -7.5)$

   _____

   _____

4. Original: $A(-2, 5)$, $B(3, 7)$, $C(5, 5)$,
   $D(2, 1)$
   Image: $A'(2, -5)$, $B'(-3, -7)$,
   $C'(-5, -5)$, $D'(-2, -1)$

   _____

   _____

Choose the letter for the best answer.

5. A figure is transformed. Which best describes the transformation of the figure?

   Original: $A(7, 3)$, $B(5, -3)$, $C(3, 0)$

   Image: $A'(-7, 3)$, $B'(-5, -3)$,
   $C'(-3, 0)$

   A rotation

   B reflection

   C translation

   D dilation

6. A figure is transformed. Which best describes the transformation of the figure?

   Original: $A(4, 8)$, $B(6, 4)$, $C(0, 2)$

   Image: $A'(3, 6)$, $B'(4.5, 3)$, $C'(0, 1.5)$

   F rotation

   G reflection

   H translation

   J dilation

7. Which coordinate map describes a 90° counterclockwise rotation?

   A $(x, y) \rightarrow (x, -y)$

   B $(x, y) \rightarrow (y, -x)$

   C $(x, y) \rightarrow (-y, x)$

   D $(x, y) \rightarrow (-x, y)$

8. Which transformation would not necessarily result in a congruent figure?

   F rotation

   G reflection

   H translation

   J dilation

Holt McDougal Mathematics

LESSON	**Geometric Relationships**
8	**Problem Solving: Identifying Combined Transformations**

For each sequence of transformations, find the coordinates of the final image and state whether the two figures are similar or congruent.

1. Original *ABC*: *A*(–3, 1), *B*(–1, 5), *C*(1, 1)

   A reflection across the *y*-axis, followed by a 90° clockwise rotation around the origin.

   _____

2. Original *ABCD*: *A*(6, –3), *B*(2, –2), *C*(–1, –2), *D*(–5, –1)

   A 180° rotation around the origin, followed by a dilation by a scale factor of 0.5, with the origin as the center of dilation.

   _____

Identify the combined transformations from the original to the final image. Tell whether the two figures are similar or congruent. Justify your answer.

3. Original *ABCDE* with *A*(–2, 2), *B*(0, 3), *C*(1, 2), *D*(1, 0), *E*(–1, 1)

   Final Image: *A″B″C″D″E″* with *A″*(–4, –6), *B″*(–5, –4), *C″*(–4, –3), *D″*(–2, –3), *E″*(–3, –5)

   _____

4. Original *ABC* with *A*(–6, –4), *B*(3, 6), *C*(3, –4)

   Final Image: *A″B″C″* with *A″*(10, –9), *B″*(1, 1), *C″*(1, –9)

   _____

5. Original *ABCD* with *A*(0, 1), *B*(1, 2), *C*(3, 0), *D*(2, –1)

   Final Image: *A″B″C″D″* with *A″*(2, 2), *B″*(1, 3), *C″*(–1, 3), *D″*(0, 0)

   _____

6. Original *ABCD* with *A*(0, 1), *B*(2, 1), *C*(2, –4), *D*(0, –4)

   Final Image: *A″B″C″D″* with *A″*(1.5, 0), *B″*(1.5, –3), *C″*(–6, –3), *D″*(–6, 0)

   _____

Choose the letter for the best answer.

7. What are the coordinates of the image of the point (2, –4) after a reflection across the *x*-axis followed by a rotation of 90° counter-clockwise around the origin?

   A (–4, –2)

   B (–4, 2)

   C (4, –2)

   D (4, 2)

8. What are the coordinates of the image of the point (–2, 1) after being dilated by a scale factor of 3 with the origin set as the center of dilation and then translated 2 units left and 3 units up?

   F (–3, 1)

   G (–6, 3)

   H (–4, 0)

   J (–1, 7)

© Houghton Mifflin Harcourt Publishing Company

Holt McDougal Mathematics

Name _____ Date _____ Class_____

LESSON 1 Measurement and Geometry
Problem Solving: Circles

Round to the nearest tenth. Use 3.14 for π. Write the correct answer.

1. The world's tallest Ferris wheel is in Osaka, Japan, and stands 369 feet tall. Its wheel has a diameter of 328 feet. Find the circumference of the Ferris wheel.

   _____

2. A dog is on a 15-foot chain that is anchored to the ground. How much area can the dog cover while he is on the chain?

   _____

3. A small pizza has a diameter of 10 inches, and a medium has a diameter of 12 inches. How much more pizza do you get with the medium pizza?

   _____

4. How much more crust do you get with a medium pizza with a diameter of 12 inches than a small pizza with a 10 inch diameter?

   _____

Round to the nearest tenth. Use 3.14 for π. Choose the letter for the best answer.

5. The wrestling mat for college NCAA competition has a wrestling circle with a diameter of 32 feet, while a high school mat has a diameter of 28 feet. How much more area is there in a college wrestling mat than a high school mat?

   A 12.6 ft^2

   B 188.4 ft^2

   C 234.8 ft^2

   D 753.6 ft^2

6. Many tire manufacturers guarantee their tires for 50,000 miles. If a tire has a 16-inch radius, how many revolutions of the tire are guaranteed? There are 63,360 inches in a mile. Round to the nearest revolution.

   F 630.6 revolutions

   G 3125 revolutions

   H 31,528,662 revolutions

   J 500,000,000 revolutions

7. In men's Olympic discus throwing competition, an athlete throws a discus with a diameter of 8.625 inches. What is the circumference of the discus?

   A 13.5 in.

   B 27.1 in.

   C 58.4 in.

   D 233.6 in.

8. An athlete in a discus competition throws from a circle that is approximately 8.2 feet in diameter. What is the area of the discus throwing circle?

   F 52.8 ft^2

   G 25.7 ft^2

   H 12.9 ft^2

   J 211.1 ft^2

 Holt McDougal Mathematics

LESSON	**Measurement and Geometry**
2	**Problem Solving: Volume of Prisms and Cylinders**

Round to the nearest tenth. Write the correct answer.

1. A contractor pours a sidewalk that is 4 inches deep, 1 yard wide, and 20 yards long. How many cubic yards of concrete will be needed? (Hint: 36 inches = 1 yard.)

   _____

2. A refrigerator has inside measurements of 50 cm by 118 cm by 44 cm. What is the capacity of the refrigerator?

   _____

A rectangular box is 2 inches high, 3.5 inches wide and 4 inches long. A cylindrical box is 3.5 inches high and has a diameter of 3.2 inches. Use 3.14 for π. Round to the nearest tenth.

3. Which box has a larger volume?

   _____

4. How much bigger is the larger box?

   _____

Use 3.14 for π. Choose the letter for the best answer.

5. A child's wading pool has a diameter of 5 feet and a height of 1 foot. How much water would it take to fill the pool? Round to the nearest gallon. (Hint: 1 cubic foot of water is approximately 7.5 gallons.)

   A 79 gallons   C 59 gallons

   B 589 gallons   D 147 gallons

6. How many cubic feet of air are in a room that is 15 feet long, 10 feet wide and 8 feet high?

   F 33 ft^3

   G 1200 ft^3

   H 1500 ft^3

   J 3768 ft^3

7. How many gallons of water will the water trough hold? Round to the nearest gallon. (Hint: 1 cubic foot of water is approximately 7.5 gallons.)

   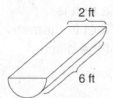

   2 ft

   6 ft

   A 19 gallons   C 141 gallons

   B 71 gallons   D 565 gallons

8. A can has diameter of 9.8 cm and is 13.2 cm tall. What is the capacity of the can? Round to the nearest tenth.

   F 203.1 cm^3

   G 995.2 cm^3

   H 3980.7 cm^3

   J 959.2 cm^3

Name _____ Date _____ Class_____

Measurement and Geometry
Problem Solving: Volume of Pyramids and Cones

Round to the nearest tenth. Use 3.14 for π. Write the correct answer.

1. The Feathered Serpent Pyramid is located in Teotihuacan, Mexico. Its base is a square that measures 65 m on each side. The pyramid is 19.4 m high. What is the volume of the Feathered Serpent Pyramid?

2. The Sun Pyramid in Teotihuacan, Mexico, is larger than the Feathered Serpent Pyramid. The sides of the square base and the height are each about 3.3 times larger than the Feathered Serpent Pyramid. How many times larger is the volume of the Sun Pyramid than the Feathered Serpent Pyramid?

_____

3. An oil funnel is in the shape of a cone. It has a diameter of 4 inches and a height of 6 inches. If the end of the funnel is plugged, how much oil can the funnel hold before it overflows?

4. One quart of oil has a volume of approximately 57.6 in^3. Does the oil funnel in exercise 3 hold more or less than 1 quart of oil?

_____

Round to the nearest tenth. Use 3.14 for π. Choose the letter for the best answer.

5. An ice cream cone has a diameter of 4.2 cm and a height of 11.5 cm. What is the volume of the cone?

   A 18.7 cm^3

   B 25.3 cm^3

   C 53.1 cm^3

   D 212.3 cm^3

6. When decorating a cake, the frosting is put into a cone-shaped bag and then squeezed out a hole at the tip of the cone. How much frosting is in a bag that has a radius of 1.5 inches and a height of 8.5 inches?

   F 5.0 in^3 H 15.2 in^3

   G 13.3 in^3 J 20.0 in^3

7. What is the volume of the hourglass at the right?

   A 13.1 in^3

   B 26.2 in^3

   C 52.3 in^3

   D 102.8 in^3

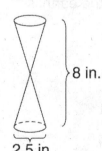

8 in.

2.5 in.

Holt McDougal Mathematics

LESSON 4 Measurement and Geometry
Problem Solving: Spheres

Early golf balls were smooth spheres. Later it was discovered that golf balls flew better when they were dimpled. On January 1, 1932, the United States Golf Association set standards for the weight and size of a golf ball. The minimum diameter of a regulation golf ball is 1.680 inches. Use 3.14 for π. Round to the nearest hundredth.

1. Find the volume of a smooth golf ball with the minimum diameter allowed by the United States Golf Association.

   _____

2. Find the surface area of a smooth golf ball with the minimum diameter allowed by the United States Golf Association.

   _____

3. Would the dimples on a golf ball increase or decrease the volume of the ball?

   _____

4. Would the dimples on a golf ball increase or decrease the surface area of the ball?

   _____

Use 3.14 for π. Use the following information for Exercises 5–6. A track and field expert recommends changes to the size of a shot put. One recommendation is that a shot put should have a diameter between 90 and 110 mm. Choose the letter for the best answer.

5. Find the surface area of a shot put with a diameter of 90 mm.

   A 25,434 mm^2

   B 101,736 mm^2

   C 381,520 mm^2

   D 3,052,080 mm^2

6. Find the surface area of a shot put with diameter 110 mm.

   F 9,499 mm^2

   G 22,834 mm^2

   H 37,994 mm^2

   J 151,976 mm^2

7. Find the volume of the earth if the average diameter of the earth is 7926 miles.

   A 2.0×10^8 mi^3

   B 2.6×10^{11} mi^3

   C 7.9×10^8 mi^3

   D 2.1×10^{12} mi^3

8. An ice cream cone has a diameter of 4.2 cm and a height of 11.5 cm. One spherical scoop of ice cream is put on the cone that has a diameter of 5.6 cm. If the ice cream were to melt in the cone, how much of it would overflow the cone? Round to the nearest tenth.

   F 0 cm^3 H 38.8 cm^3

   G 12.3 cm^3 J 54.3 cm^3

LESSON 1

Multi-Step Equations

Problem Solving: Simplifying Algebraic Expressions

Write the correct answer.

1. An item costs x dollars. The tax rate is 5% of the cost of the item, or $0.05x$. Write and simplify an expression to find the total cost of the item with tax.

2. A sweater costs d dollars at regular price. The sweater is reduced by 20%, or $0.2d$. Write and simplify an expression to find the cost of the sweater before tax.

3. Consecutive integers are integers that differ by one. You can represent consecutive integers as x, $x + 1$, $x + 2$ and so on. Write an equation and solve to find three consecutive integers whose sum is 33.

4. Consecutive even integers can be represented by x, $x + 2$, $x + 4$ and so on. Write an equation and solve to find three consecutive even integers whose sum is 54.

Choose the letter for the best answer.

5. In Super Bowl XXXV, the total number of points scored was 41. The winning team outscored the losing team by 27 points. What was the final score of the game?

    A 33 to 8

    B 34 to 7

    C 22 to 2

    D 18 to 6

6. A high school basketball court is 34 feet longer than it is wide. If the perimeter of the court is 268, what are the dimensions of the court?

    F 234 ft by 34 ft

    G 67 ft by 67 ft

    H 70 ft by 36 ft

    J 84 ft by 50 ft

7. Julia ordered 2 hamburgers and Steven ordered 3 hamburgers. If their total bill before tax was $7.50, how much did each hamburger cost?

    A $1.50

    B $1.25

    C $1.15

    D $1.02

8. On three tests, a student scored a total of 258 points. If the student improved his performance on each test by 5 points, what was the score on each test?

    F 81, 86, 91

    G 80, 85, 90

    H 75, 80, 85

    J 70, 75, 80

LESSON	# Multi-Step Equations
2	## Problem Solving: Solving Multi-Step Equations

A taxi company charges $2.25 for the first mile and then $0.20 per mile for each mile after the first, or $F = \$2.25 + \$0.20(m - 1)$ where F is the fare and m is the number of miles.

1. If Juan's taxi fare was $6.05, how many miles did he travel in the taxi?

   _____

2. If Juan's taxi fare was $7.65, how many miles did he travel in the taxi?

   _____

A new car loses 20% of its original value when you buy it and then 8% of its original value per year, or $D = 0.8V - 0.08Vy$ where D is the value after y years with an original value V.

3. If a vehicle that was valued at $20,000 new is now worth $9,600, how old is the car?

   _____

4. A 6-year old vehicle is worth $12,000. What was the original value of the car?

   _____

The equation used to estimate typing speed is $S = \dfrac{1}{5}(w - 10e)$, where S is the accurate typing speed, w is the number of words typed in 5 minutes and e is the number of errors. Choose the letter of the best answer.

5. Jane can type 55 words per minute (wpm). In 5 minutes, she types 285 words. How many errors would you expect her to make?

   A 0   C 2

   B 1   D 5

6. If Alex types 300 words in 5 minutes with 5 errors, what is his typing speed?

   F 48 wpm   H 59 wpm

   G 50 wpm   J 60 wpm

7. Johanna receives a report that says her typing speed is 65 words per minute. She knows that she made 4 errors in the 5-minute test. How many words did she type in 5 minutes?

   A 285   C 365

   B 329   D 1825

8. Cecil can type 35 words per minute. In 5 minutes, she types 255 words. How many errors would you expect her to make?

   F 2   H 6

   G 4   J 8

LESSON
3

Multi-Step Equations

Problem Solving: Solving Equations with Variables on Both Sides

The chart below describes three long-distance calling plans.
Round to the nearest minute. Write the correct answer.

1. For what number of minutes will
   plan A and plan B cost the same?

   _____

Long-Distance Plans

Plan	Monthly Access Fee	Charge per minute
A	$3.95	$0.08
B	$8.95	$0.06
C	$0	$0.10

2. For what number of minutes per month
   will plan B and plan C cost the same?

   _____

3. For what number of minutes will plan A
   and plan C cost the same?

   _____

Choose the letter for the best answer.

4. Carpet Plus installs carpet for $100
   plus $8 per square yard of carpet.
   Carpet World charges $75 for
   installation and $10 per square yard
   of carpet. Find the number of square
   yards of carpet for which the cost
   including carpet and installation is
   the same.

   A 1.4 yd^2 C 12.5 yd^2

   B 9.7 yd^2 D 87.5 yd^2

5. One shuttle service charges $10 for
   pickup and $0.10 per mile. The other
   shuttle service has no pickup fee but
   charges $0.35 per mile. Find the
   number of miles for which the cost of
   the shuttle services is the same.

   F 2.5 miles

   G 22 miles

   H 40 miles

   J 48 miles

6. Joshua can purchase tile at one
   store for $0.99 per tile, but he will
   have to rent a tile saw for $25. At
   another store he can buy tile for
   $1.50 per tile and borrow a tile saw
   for free. Find the number of tiles for
   which the cost is the same. Round
   to the nearest tile.

   A 10 tiles   C 25 tiles

   B 13 tiles   D 49 tiles

7. One plumber charges a fee of
   $75 per service call plus $15 per
   hour. Another plumber has no flat
   fee, but charges $25 per hour. Find
   the number of hours for which the
   cost of the two plumbers is the same.

   F 2.1 hours   H 7.5 hours

   G 7 hours   J 7.8 hours

Multi-Step Equations

Problem Solving: Systems of Equations

After college, Julia is offered two different jobs. The table summarizes the pay offered with each job. Write the correct answer.

1. Write an equation that shows the pay y of Job A after x years.

   _____

Job	Yearly Salary	Yearly Increase
A	$20,000	$2500
B	$25,000	$2000

2. Write an equation that shows the pay y of Job B after x years.

   _____

3. Is (8, 35,000) a solution to the system of equations in Exercises 1 and 2?

   _____

4. Solve the system of equations in Exercises 1 and 2.

   _____

5. If Julia plans to stay at this job only a few years and pay is the only consideration, which job should she choose?

   _____

A travel agency is offering two Orlando trip plans that include hotel accommodations and pairs of tickets to theme parks. Use the table below. Choose the letter for the best answer.

6. Find an equation about trip A where x represents the hotel cost per night and y represents the cost per pair of theme park tickets.

   A $5x + 2y = 415$ C $8x + 6y = 415$

   B $2x + 3y = 415$ D $3x + 2y = 415$

Trip	Number of nights	Pairs of theme park tickets	Cost
A	3	2	$415
B	5	4	$725

7. Find an equation about trip B where x represents the hotel cost per night and y represents the cost per pair of theme park tickets.

   F $5x + 4y = 725$

   G $4x + 5y = 725$

   H $8x + 6y = 725$

   J $3x + 4y = 725$

8. Solve the system of equations to find the nightly hotel cost and the cost for each pair of theme park tickets.

   A ($50, $105)

   B ($125, $20)

   C ($105, $50)

   D ($115, $35)

Graphing Lines

LESSON 1

Problem Solving: Graphing Linear Equations

Write the correct answer.

1. The distance in feet traveled by a falling object is found by the formula $d = 16t^2$ where d is the distance in feet and t is the time in seconds. Graph the equation. Is the equation linear?

   _____

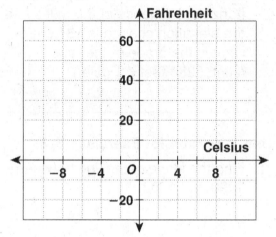

2. The formula that relates Celsius to Fahrenheit is $F = \dfrac{9}{5}C + 32$. Graph the equation. Is the equation linear?

   _____

Wind chill is the temperature that the air feels like with the effect of the wind. The graph below shows the wind chill equation for a wind speed of 25 mph. For Exercises 3–6, refer to the graph.

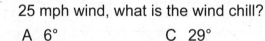

3. If the temperature is 40° with a 25 mph wind, what is the wind chill?

   A 6°   C 29°

   B 20°   D 40°

4. If the temperature is 20° with a 25 mph wind, what is the wind chill?

   F 3°   H 13°

   G 10°   J 20°

5. If the temperature is 0° with a 25 mph wind, what is the wind chill?

   A −30°   C −15°

   B −24°   D 0°

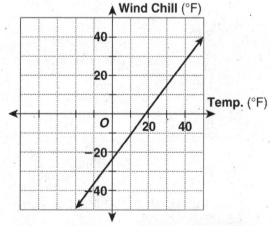

6. If the wind chill is 10° and there is a 25 mph wind, what is the actual temperature?

   F −11°   H 15°

   G 0°   J 25°

Name _____ Date _____ Class_____

Graphing Lines

Problem Solving: Slope of a Line

Write the correct answer.

1. The state of Kansas has a fairly steady slope from the east to the west. At the eastern side, the elevation is 771 ft. At the western edge, 413 miles across the state, the elevation is 4039 ft. What is the approximate slope of Kansas?

2. The Feathered Serpent Pyramid in Teotihuacan, Mexico, has a square base. From the center of the base to the center of an edge of the pyramid is 32.5 m. The pyramid is 19.4 m high. What is the slope of each triangular face of the pyramid?

3. On a highway, a 6% grade means a slope of 0.06. If a highway covers a horizontal distance of 0.5 miles and the elevation change is 184.8 feet, what is the grade of the road? (Hint: 5280 feet = 1 mile.)

4. The roof of a house rises vertically 3 feet for every 12 feet of horizontal distance. What is the slope, or pitch of the roof?

Use the graph for Exercises 5–8.

5. Find the slope of the line between 1990 and 1992.

   A $\dfrac{2}{11}$ C $\dfrac{11}{2}$

   B $\dfrac{35}{3982}$ D $\dfrac{11}{1992}$

6. Find the slope of the line between 1994 and 1996.

   F $\dfrac{7}{2}$ H $\dfrac{2}{7}$

   G $\dfrac{37}{3990}$ J $\dfrac{7}{1996}$

7. Find the slope of the line between 1998 and 2000.

   A 1   C $\dfrac{1}{1000}$

   B $\dfrac{1}{999}$ D 2

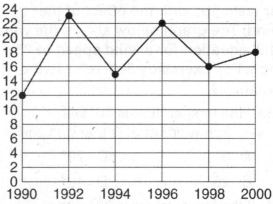

Number of Earthquakes Worldwide with a Magnitude of 7.0 or Greater

8. What does it mean when the slope is negative?

   F The number of earthquakes stayed the same.

   G The number of earthquakes increased.

   H The number of earthquakes decreased.

   J It means nothing.

Holt McDougal Mathematics

LESSON 3 Graphing Lines
Problem Solving: Using Slopes and Intercepts

Write the correct answer.

1. Jaime purchased a $20 bus pass. Each time she rides the bus, $1.25 is deducted from the pass. The linear equation $y = -1.25x + 20$ represents the amount of money on the bus pass after x rides. Identify the slope and the x- and y-intercepts. Graph the equation at the right.

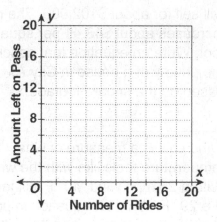

_____

_____

2. The rent charged for space in an office building is related to the size of the space rented. The rent for 600 square feet of floor space is $750, while the rent for 900 square feet is $1150. Write an equation for the rent y based on the square footage of the floor space x.

_____

Choose the letter of the correct answer.

3. A limousine charges $35 plus $2 per mile. Which equation shows the total cost of a ride in the limousine?

  A $y = 35x + 2$ C $y = 2x - 35$

  B $y = 2x + 35$ D $2x + 35y = 2$

4. A newspaper delivery person earns $75 each day plus $0.10 per paper delivered. Which equation shows the daily earnings of a delivery person?

  F $y = 0.1x + 75$ H $x + 0.1y = 75$

  G $y = 75x + 0.1$ J $0.1x + y = 75$

5. A friend gave Ms. Morris a $50 gift card for a local car wash. If each car wash costs $6, which equation shows the number of dollars left on the card?

  A $50x + 6y = 1$ C $y = -6x + 50$

  B $y = 6x + 50$ D $y = 6x - 50$

6. Antonio's weekly allowance is given by the equation $A = 0.5c + 10$, where c is the number of chores he does. If he received $16 in allowance one week, how many chores did he do?

  F 10   H 14

  G 12   J 15

LESSON **Graphing Lines**

4 **Problem Solving: Point-Slope Form**

Write the correct answer.

1. A 1600 square foot home in City A will sell for about $102,000. The price increases about $43.41 per square foot. Write an equation that describes the price y of a house in City A, based on the square footage x.

_____

2. Write the equation in Exercise 1 in slope-intercept form.

_____

3. Wind chill is a measure of what temperature feels like with the wind. With a 25 mph wind, 40 °F will feel like 29 °F. Write an equation in point-slope form that describes the wind chill y based on the temperature x, if the slope of the line is 1.337.

_____

4. With a 25 mph wind, what does a temperature of 0 °F feel like?

_____

From 2 to 13 years, the growth rate for children is generally linear. Choose the letter of the correct answer.

5. The average height of a 2-year old boy is 36 inches, and the average growth rate per year is 2.2 inches. Write an equation in point-slope form that describes the height of a boy y based on his age x.

  A $y - 36 = 2(x - 2.2)$

  B $y - 2 = 2.2(x - 36)$

  C $y - 36 = 2.2(x - 2)$

  D $y - 2.2 = 2(x - 36)$

6. The average height of a 5-year old girl is 44 inches, and the average growth rate per year is 2.4 inches. Write an equation in point-slope form that describes the height of a girl y based on her age x.

  F $y - 2.4 = 44(x - 5)$

  G $y - 44 = 2.4(x - 5)$

  H $y - 44 = 5(x - 2.4)$

  J $y - 5 = 2.4(x - 44)$

7. Write the equation from Exercise 6 in slope-intercept form.

  A $y = 2.4x - 100.6$

  B $y = 44x - 217.6$

  C $y = 5x + 32$

  D $y = 2.4x + 32$

8. Use the equation in Exercise 6 to find the average height of a 13-year old girl.

  F 56.3 in.

  G 63.2 in.

  H 69.4 in.

  J 97 in.

© Houghton Mifflin Harcourt Publishing Company

Graphing Lines

LESSON 5

Problem Solving: Direct Variation

Determine whether the data sets show direct variation. If so, find the equation of direct variation.

1. The table shows the distance in feet traveled by a falling object in certain times. $y = kx$

Time (s)	0	0.5	1	1.5	2	2.5	3
Distance (ft)	0	4	16	36	64	100	144

no

_____

_____

2. The R-value of insulation gives the material's resistance to heat flow. The table shows the R-value for different thicknesses of fiberglass insulation.

Thickness (in.)	1	2	3	4	5	6
R-value	3.14	6.28	9.42	12.56	15.7	18.84

yes

$y = 3.14x$

3. The table shows the lifting power of hot air.

Hot Air (ft³)	50	100	500	1000	2000	3000
Lift (lb)	1	2	10	20	40	60

_____

_____

4. The table shows the relationship between degrees Celsius and degrees Fahrenheit.

° Celsius	−10	−5	0	5	10	20	30
° Fahrenheit	14	23	32	41	50	68	86

_____

_____

Your weight on Earth varies directly with your weights on other planetary bodies. The table below shows how much a person who weighs 100 lb on Earth would weigh on the moon and different planets.

5. Find the equation of direct variation for the weight on earth e and on the moon m.

A $m = 0.166e$ C $m = 6.02e$

B $m = 16.6e$ D $m = 1660e$

Planetary Bodies	Weight (lb)
Moon	16.6
Jupiter	236.4
Pluto	6.7

6. How much would a 150 lb person weigh on Jupiter?

F 63.5 lb   H 354.6 lb

G 286.4 lb   J 483.7 lb

7. How much would a 150 lb person weigh on Pluto?

A 5.8 lb   C 12.3 lb

B 10.05 lb   D 2238.8 lb

Graphing Lines

LESSON 6

Problem Solving: Solving Systems of Linear Equations by Graphing

Write the equations for each system. Graph the system to solve each problem.

Kelly needs to order lunch for the 6 people at a business meeting. Her menu choices are chicken salad for a cost of $5 per person and egg salad for a cost of $4 per person. She only has $28 to spend. More people want chicken salad. How many of each lunch can she order?

1. Write one equation in a system for this situation. _____

2. Write a second equation in the system.

   _____

3. What do x and y represent?

   _____

   _____

4. How many of each type of lunch can she order?

   _____

   _____

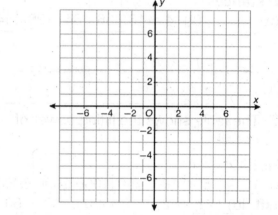

Solve each problem.

5. How many solutions does this system have?

$$y = -3x + 6$$
$$9x + 3y = 18$$

   A 0   C 2

   B 1   D infinite

6. How many solutions does this system have?

$$5x - y = 1$$
$$2x = 3y$$

   F 0   H 2

   G 1   J infinite

7. For which system is the ordered pair (2, –2) a solution?

  A
$$y = x$$
$$y = \frac{1}{2}x - 3$$

  C
$$y = -x$$
$$y = \frac{1}{2}x - 3$$

  B
$$y = -\frac{1}{2}x$$
$$y = 2x - 4$$

  D
$$2y = -x$$
$$2y = 2x$$

8. Which is the best description for the graph of this system of equations?

$$x + y = 4 \quad y = -x + y$$
$$4x + 4y = 8 \quad y = -x + 2$$

  F same line

  G parallel lines

  H intersecting lines

  J coinciding lines

Holt McDougal Mathematics

Data, Prediction, and Linear Functions

LESSON 1

Problem Solving: Scatter Plots

Use the data given at the right.

1. Make a scatter plot of the data.

Percent of Americans Who Have Completed High School

Year	Percent
1910	13.5
1920	16.4
1930	19.1
1940	24.5
1950	34.3
1960	41.1
1970	55.2
1980	68.6
1990	77.6
1999	83.4

2. Does the data show a positive, negative or no correlation?

_____

3. Use the scatter plot to predict the percent of Americans who will complete high school in 2010.

_____

Choose the letter for the best answer.

4. Which data sets have a positive correlation?

A The length of the lines at amusement park rides and the number of rides you can ride in a day

B The temperature on a summer day and the number of visitors at a swimming pool

C The square miles of a state and the population of the state in the 2000 census

D The length of time spent studying and doing homework and the length of time spent doing other activities

5. Which data sets have a negative correlation?

F The number of visitors at an amusement park and the length of the lines for the rides

G The amount of speed over the speed limit when you get a speeding ticket and the amount of the fine for speeding

H The temperature and the number of people wearing coats

J The distance you live from school and the amount of time it takes to get to school

Holt McDougal Mathematics

LESSON	**Data, Prediction, and Linear Functions**
2	**Problem Solving: Linear Best Fit Models**

Use the scatter plot for Exercises 1–3.

1. Does the pattern of association between time studied and score appear to be linear or nonlinear?

   _____

2. Describe the correlation between the time studied and the scores as positive, negative, or no correlation.

   _____

3. Identify any possible outliers.

   _____

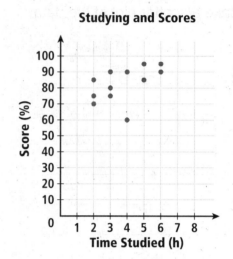

Studying and Scores

Choose the letter for the best answer. Use the scatter plot for Exercises 4–6.

4. What does the point (0, 400) represent in this scatter plot?

   A the temperature at an elevation of 0 feet

   B the elevation at a temperature of 58°F

   C the elevation at a temperature of 0°F

   D the temperature at an elevation of 500 feet

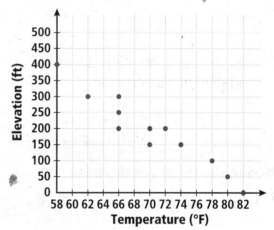

Temperatures and Elevation

5. Which best describes the correlation between the temperatures and the elevations in the scatter plot?

   F strong positive

   G weak positive

   H strong negative

   J weak negative

6. Which equation best represents the line of best fit?

   A $y = -16x + 400$

   B $y = -15x + 300$

   C $y = 15x - 300$

   D $y = 16x - 400$

Data, Prediction, and Linear Functions

LESSON 3

LESSON 4 Problem Solving: Linear Functions

Write the correct answer.

1. On April 14–15, 1921 in Silver Lake, Colorado, 76 inches of snow fell in 24 hours, at an average rate of 3.2 inches per hour. Find a rule for the linear function that describes the amount of snow after x hours at the average rate.

2. At the average rate of snowfall from Exercise 1, how much snow had fallen in 15 hours?

3. The altitude of clouds in feet can be found by multiplying the difference between the temperature and the dew point by 228. If the temperature is 75°, find a rule for the linear function that describes the height of the clouds with dew point x.

4. If the temperature is 75° and the dew point is 40°, what is the height of the clouds?

For Exercises 5–7, refer to the table below, which shows the relationship between the number of times a cricket chirps in a minute and temperature.

5. Find a rule for the linear function that describes the temperature based on x, the number of cricket chirps in a minute based on temperature.

A $f(x) = x + 5$

B $f(x) = \dfrac{x}{4} + 40$

C $f(x) = x - 20$

D $f(x) = \dfrac{x}{2} + 20$

Cricket Chirps/min	Temperature (°F)
80	60
100	65
120	70
140	75

6. What is the temperature if a cricket chirps 150 times in a minute?

F 77.5 °F   H 130 °F

G 95 °F   J 155 °F

7. If the temperature is 85 °F, how many times will a cricket chirp in a minute?

A 61   C 180

B 105   D 200

Holt McDougal Mathematics

<table>
<tr><td>LESSON
4</td><td># Data, Prediction, and Linear Functions
Problem Solving: Comparing Multiple Representations</td></tr>
</table>

**Find and compare the rates of change and initial values of the
linear functions in terms of the situations they model.**

1. Dan and Keri assemble bicycles.
   So far today, Dan has assembled
   3 bikes. He works at a rate of 0.5
   bikes per hour. Keri has assembled
   4 bikes, so far today, and assembles
   bicycles as shown in the table.

Time (hr)	0	1	2	3
Bikes Keri Assembled	4	4.75	5.5	6.25

_____

_____

_____

2. Javier and Wendy pay for their cell
   phone service from their checking
   accounts according to the equation
   and graph shown.
   Javier: $f(x) = -65x + 450$
   Wendy

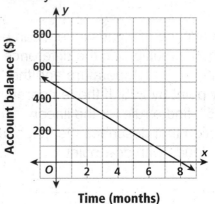

Time (months)

_____

_____

_____

**Use the table and the graph for Exercises 3 and 4. Choose the
letter for the best answer.**

Jane and Alex each start driving from their homes, which
are different distances from the warehouse where they
both work, to a meeting out of town.

Alex

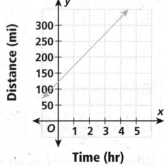

Time (hr)

Jane

Time (hr)	2	3	4	5
Distance (mi)	185	240	295	350

3. How much farther from the
   warehouse was Jane than Alex
   when she started driving today?

   A 50 miles   C 75 miles

   B 60 miles   D 200 miles

4. How much faster is Jane driving
   than Alex?

   A 55 miles per hour

   B 50 miles per hour

   C 25 miles per hour

   D 5 miles per hour

Holt McDougal Mathematics